eBay 2014

Why You're Not Selling Anything on eBay,
and What You Can Do About It

Contact me at

E-mail: hi@nickvulich.com
Blog: indieauthorstoolbox.com

Amazon Author Page:

- amazon.com/author/nickvulich
- amazon.com/author/nicholasvulich

Why you need to read this book

One thing I've found in fourteen years of selling on eBay is the market is always changing, and just when you think you've got it all figured out, either eBay comes along and changes the rules of the game, or the economy changes, and your niche implodes, sending your sales straight down the toilet.

One of the biggest things you're going to have to deal with is eBay's unending string of changes. As I'm writing this, eBay has just announced some of their fall changes, and let me tell you – the entire year has been a crazy roller coaster ride for eBay sellers.

The 2013 Spring Seller Update raised store subscription fees for most sellers.

Here's the reality:

Basic Store

. Fee increases from $15.99 to 19.99 per month

. 150 free listings (fixed price or auction)

. 20 cents for each fixed price listing

. 25 cents for each auction listing

Premium store

. Fee increases from $49.99 to $59.99 per month

. 500 free listings (fixed price or auction)

. 10 cents for each fixed price listing

. 15 cents for each auction listing

Anchor Store

. Fee increases from $179.99 to 199.99 per month

. 2500 free listings (fixed price or auction)

. 5 cents for each fixed price listing

. 10 cents for each auction listing

The 2013 Fall Seller Update was just released as I'm writing this. The good news is – there are no crazy changes on the horizon for sellers with this one. If you haven't checked it out yet, follow this link to read more:
http://pages.ebay.com/sellerinformation/news/fallupdate2013/overview.html

Here are the highlights from that update:

1) Additional top rated seller grace period. If you fall below the requirements eBay is going to give you an additional two months to move back into compliance. This way a bad sales month or one time bad feedback isn't going to affect your status and discounts.

2) Expanded feedback removal policy. What this means is eBay is going to be more proactive in protecting your feedback rating. If you receive negative or neutral feedback from a seller who did not pay, was suspended, or is a habitual leaver of bad feedback, eBay will automatically remove the negative feedback for you.

Weather related feedback or circumstances that are out of your control will also be looked at in removing negative feedback.

The update also outlines the process for requesting eBay to remove negative feedback.

3) eBay managed returns have been streamlined and the policy for them updated. Key take a-ways: They are going to allow more time for returns, and return shipping is guaranteed to be no more than what you originally charged for shipping.

4) Item specific changes are being implemented in several categories. To see how the changes may affect you visit this link: http://pages.ebay.com/sellerinformation/news/fallupdate2013/categoryupdates.html.

Outside of eBay's seller updates, there have been numerous other issues affecting sellers this year. One of the most stressful ones is having your sales come to a dead stop.

Many sellers liken the experience to eBay shutting the faucet off, and then turning it back on at a later date. If you haven't experienced it yet, you soon may. And, the crazy thing is it comes in waves. You can sell twenty items in two days, and then your sales stop dead for a week or ten days. Then the faucet is turned back on and you get another two or three days of sales, before the cycle repeats itself.

Sellers affected by these shutdowns get a sinking hopeless feeling in their stomachs, because no matter what they try (lowering prices, offering free shipping, or refreshing listings) nothing seems to work.

Believe me, I've been there a lot, and it's not a good feeling.

So, what do you do?

I've been following all of the forums and blogs on this topic and here's what I've found out.

Cassini Search does not play well with html, especially when the html code is at the top of the listing information. What that means for sellers is if you have a designer heading in your eBay listings, it may be negatively impacting your sales. One seller on Ecommerce Bytes Blog reported the phenomena occurring with his listings. After much testing he discovered when he eliminated the header from his listings, sales resumed at their normal pace.

So if you are one of the sellers affected by eBay's leaky faucet my suggestion would be to examine your listings and remove any offending html code.

Html code has also been found to play havoc with mobile listing on eBay. It seems that if your listing has any html code or embedded pictures in it, eBay often times will not include it in mobile search.

First let me frame what this means for sellers. Right now roughly thirty-five percent of online sales occur on cell phones or mobile devices such as iPads and Android tablets. This number is soon expected to exceed fifty percent. So if your items don't come up in mobile search, you're missing out on a minimum of fifty percent of your sales potential.

Best practices suggest you need to take a hard look at all of your eBay listings and decide what's more important: Looking good, or selling more product?

I've examined a large number of my listings using the eBay Mobile App and I've been able to pull most of them up on my Android phone. Most of the items listed with templates from Auctiva, Ink Frog, etc. create particular difficulties for eBay buyers. In most cases buyers can view only one picture, even if you have four to six embedded pictures in the listing. Sometimes when you select description the original listing will come up in its original format, sometimes it won't.

The other key takeaway involving pictures is if you post them through eBay's system, buyers can just click the arrow next to the first picture and it expands to fill the whole screen so they can page through pictures one at a time. It offers buyers a better shopping experience with big clear pictures. If you use a template, or embed pictures, you don't have this option. Your gallery picture is the only one that will be displayed.

One work around if you must use a template is to upload your pictures twice. Embed them in your template, but also upload them in eBay's picture tool. This way you have the best of both worlds.

Enough said. Think really hard before you decide to continue using listing templates. If your sales are down, consider relisting your items without any templates, headers, or embedded pictures and record how it impacts your sales. This way you can make an informed decision about what works best for you.

Another work around sellers have found for slumping sales is to rework their existing listings. What I'm saying here is many sellers have thousands of items packed away in their eBay stores that are neither selling nor getting page views. Especially with collectibles and book sellers, the goal is to list as many items on the site as possible and wait for the right buyer to come along.

Some sellers have suggested eBay has an internal timer running on your listings until they eventually consider them stale. After a certain period of time they either move them to the bottom of search results, or just stop showing them altogether. One seller talked about this on the Ecommerce Bytes Blog, and said in an effort to combat this syndrome he has been taking down his older listings and reworking them. What he's found is immediately after reworking his items they move back up in search, and his sales increase. I can vouch for this strategy. I've been using it with my own listings over the past three months, and after I rework a batch of listings, visibility and sales for those items skyrocket.

Try it for yourself and see if it helps invigorate your stale listings.

One last thing I want to talk about here is pictures. This year eBay came out with new picture requirements.

1) Every listing is required to have at least one picture, even if you are selling using the eBay catalog.

2) All pictures are required to be at least 500 pixels on the longest end; eBay suggests 1600 pixels for maximum clarity when they blow them up.

3) Text and watermarks with your logo or business name are no longer allowed in gallery pictures.

That last one has been a problem for many sellers. One example that comes to mind here is if you're selling a Calvin Klein clothing item, and you shoot a close up of the label to prove it's authentic. If you use that picture as your gallery image there's a very good chance eBay's system is going to take your listing down because it will think it has text over the image. Lesson learned, label pictures are a great addition to your listings, but don't use them for your gallery image. It's not worth the hassle.

Table of Contents

Introduction

In an ideal world, there wouldn't be any need for a book like this. Every item you list on eBay would attract hundreds of bidders That 2013 Lincoln penny you got in change this morning, and listed on eBay as soon as you got home, would be feeling the love, and drawing hundreds of dollars in bids.

Unfortunately, the sad fact is, less than forty percent of the auctions posted on eBay actually sell. Put in words just about anyone can understand **three out of five items you try to sell – Won't Sell - Period**.

Sorry to be the one to tell you that, but most of the eBay books out there make it sound like you're going to sell every item you list for sale on eBay.

Contrary to popular belief – "List it and they will buy it" is not a viable eBay strategy. Just because you decide to sell an item doesn't mean people will magically flock to it, or bid on it.

Selling on eBay is all about getting your listings noticed. No matter how unique or special the item you're selling is, no one can buy it if they can't find it.

eBay marketing can be summed up in five simple words: title, illustration, description, price, and reputation.

This book is going to help you fine tune each of these eBay marketing strategies, so you can up your odds, and have a better chance of making a sale each time you're up to bat.

1) **Title**. Hands down, your title is the number one marketing tool available to you on eBay. eBay gives you eighty-eight characters to describe your item. You need to make use of every one of them to ensure your item is visible to the largest number of viewers possible.

2) **Illustration**. You've heard the old saying "a picture is worth a thousand words." On eBay, that saying goes double. The more high quality pictures you post with your listings, the better the chances are you will sell your item, and get more money from it.

3) **Description**. A good description complements your title and illustrations. This is where you get the opportunity to drive home how great your item is, what condition it is in, and how great it would be to own one of these. Five or ten words will not cut it here. You need to tell a great story, and connect the dots, so people will understand why they need to buy your item.

4) **Price**. Your title, illustration, and description are all wasted if you place the wrong price on your item. Price your item too high, and no one will want it, price your item too low, and you will be leaving profit on the table. Pricing is part science, and part art. We will explore price in much more detail later in this guide.

5) **Reputation**. If you don't have good feedback, no one will buy from you. *On eBay, all you've got is your good name.* Face the fact: ***You're going to live and die by your feedback.*** No matter how unfair it sounds, do whatever it takes to make your customers happy.

That's really all it takes. Follow these five simple steps, and you will have a better chance of selling every item you list on eBay

We're also going to take a look at selling beyond eBay. For many sellers this can be pushing your sales out to Amazon, eBid, eCRATER, Etsy, and bidStart. Other sellers may decide to go it alone, and start their own websites. Whichever you choose, we will give you some ideas to make the transition easier.

Why listen to me?

Hey there, Nick Vulich here.

If you're like me, I'm sure you're probably a little skeptical about taking advice from someone without knowing a little bit about them first.

I've been selling on eBay since 1999. Most of my online customers know me as history-bytes, although I've also operated as its old news, back door video, and sports card one.

I've sold 30,004 items for a total of $411,755.44 over the past fifteen years, and that's just on my history-bytes id. Right now I've cut way back on eBay selling to focus on my writing, but I still keep my hat in the game. That way I can stay current with the challenges my readers face every day when they go to sell on eBay.

I've been an eBay Power Seller or Top Rated Seller for most of the past fifteen years, which means I've met eBay's sales and customer satisfaction goals.

Right off, that tells you I'm not coming at you out of left field, with all sorts of half-baked ideas I learned from reading eBay how-to books. Most of the tips I'm going to share with you, I've learned from the school of hard-knocks. I learned it from being out there selling every day, and experimenting with new products, and new listing methods.

This is the seventh book I've written about selling on eBay. The first two, *Freaking Idiots Guide to Selling on eBay*, and *eBay Unleashed*, are aimed more towards how to get started selling on eBay. *eBay 2014* is directed at more advanced sellers and tackles many of the challenges top rated sellers face in the eBay marketplace. *eBay Subject Matter Expert* suggests a different approach to selling on eBay – building a platform where customers recognize you as an expert in your niche, and buy from you because of your knowledge in that field. *Sell It Online* gives a brief overview of selling on eBay, Amazon, Etsy, and Fiver. *How to Make Money Selling Old Books & Magazines on eBay* talks specifically about what I know best, how to sell books and magazines on eBay.

Taken together these books give you all the information you need to succeed on eBay. My goal is to help you become as successful as you wish to be.

Let's get started...

What's in a title?

eBay gives you eighty-eight characters to describe your item. Your goal is to cram every last detail and keyword you can into those eighty-eight characters.

The first thing to know is your title is how people are going to find the item you're selling on eBay. eBay uses the words in your title to determine who will see your item. Because of this, it's important to have every possible word or combination of words someone might search by in the title.

Your title doesn't have to read well or even make sense to be effective. It just needs to contain as many keywords as possible to maximize the chances it will be displayed when someone searches for a similar item.

Unfortunately, many people waste this valuable space trying to get cutesy or to write a sentence that makes sense. The fact is no one is going to search for, "very nice," "awesome," "great," or "one-of-a-kind." You would be much better off giving a professional descriptor like "near-mint" or "MS65," because these are terms collectors are looking for.

Here are a few tips to help you write more effective titles:

1) **Include as many keywords as possible**. You've got eighty-eight characters. Use as many of them as you can in each title you write. Don't worry that your title doesn't make sense. Just be sure to include all of the keywords you think someone would use to describe the item you are selling.

2) **Double Check Your Spelling**. In order to get found by the maximum number of people, use proper spelling. If you're in doubt, use spell-check.

3) **Avoid using adjectives and descriptive phrases**. Save all of the adjectives and descriptive phrases for your item description. No one searches for "very nice" – "LQQK" – or "WoW!"

4) **Avoid excess capitalization**. No one likes being shouted at, or knowing someone is working too hard to sell them. If you absolutely must use all capitalization, only do it to one word, not your entire title.

5) **Use the correct terms**. If you are totally unfamiliar with the item you're selling, take a moment to Google it. One thing I've discovered over the years is people love to email you, and criticize you when you spell a word incorrectly, put an item in the wrong category, or describe it wrong. Sometimes it feels like they're crawling out of the woodwork and gunning for you personally.

6) **Include common misspellings**. If the item you're selling is frequently misspelled on eBay, include the misspellings in your title if you have room. PlayStation (paystation – plataitian - laystation)

7) **Don't use abbreviations**. Using abbreviations will normally just confuse your customers. If there is any doubt, spell it out. If you don't have room in your title for the word you want to use, chose another word with a similar meaning. The exception here would be commonly accepted abbreviations on eBay. NWT – New with tags, NIB – New in box, BNWT – Brand new with tags, FS – Factory sealed.

With all of that said, one of the hardest things for many sellers to do is decide which keywords to put in your title.

Perhaps the easiest way to decide which keywords to include in your title is to look at other auctions for similar items. How do they describe the item? What keywords do they use? What words do you see show up in all of the auctions?

After you've made the above list, take a minute to put yourself in the buyer's shoes. What words would you use to describe the item you're selling? Those are the keywords you want to include in your title.

Choosing a topic to write about

Pictures sell items.

(eBay's new rules require you to upload at least one photo with every item, even if you are using their catalog. All pictures need to be at least 500 pixels along the longest end; 1600 pixels are suggested to take maximum advantage of their picture enhancements.

Another change in the picture policy concerns watermarks, and text in pictures. You are no longer allowed to watermark you picture with your business name or logo. They also no longer allow you to include text in your galley image.)

Make no mistake about it, very few people are going to buy your item if you don't include at least one picture. More pictures are always better.

Ask yourself this, would you shell out $400 for a used laptop if you couldn't see a picture of it first?

Now what if I was selling a rare Hummel figurine and my description said it was in mint condition except for a small chip at the bottom of one leg, but I just showed one picture of the entire figurine. You'd probably have some lingering doubts about that chip, wouldn't you? As a seller, I could have easily moved you past those reservations by including several close-up pictures of the chipped area. That way you could decide for yourself, whether the chip is a bid stopper for you or not.

What you need to do is take a good look at every item you are selling. Put yourself in the buyer's shoes. What parts of the item would you need to see to decide if you want to buy that item? For a baseball card, you obviously need to see the front and back of the card. If you're selling a laptop, you probably want a picture of it with the Windows logo on the screen for proof it works. You would also want to have a picture showing any accessories you are offering with the laptop. This means cords, case, manuals, discs, and anything else included in the auction.

If you're selling clothes, be sure to take a look at how some of the bigger sellers do it. Many of them have male and female manikins they can model their clothes on. This gives potential buyers a better reference for what they are buying than just looking at a flat picture of a blouse or pair of jeans. Another thing the really good sellers do is to include close-up pictures of designs, and any flaws they have described.

Here's the advice I gave about using pictures in my other book, *Freaking Idiot's Guide to Selling on eBay*. It's still solid advice on how you should include pictures in your item descriptions.

> *You can have the best title, a great description, and a killer price, but if your pictures suck you're not likely to make a deal.*

> *When people are ready to buy something, especially expensive items, they demand great pictures. The best example you can find here is your local car dealer. They don't stop with one picture. Most often you will find twenty to twenty-five pictures for every car they are selling. Your car dealer knows most customers shop on the internet before they come in.*

> *As a result dealers give you a virtual tour of the car with the pictures they take. On the outside, they show you front, back,*

and both sides. There is at least one picture of the engine, a view into the trunk, the upper dash board, the odometer showing the mileage, the floor – front and back, and close ups of any damage.

You can learn a lot about the type of pictures you need by studying car dealers listings. The lighting is always perfect. Every picture is perfectly centered. They never put in a bad picture. They know one bad picture can kill the whole deal.

Plan your pictures the same way. You want at least one overall view of your item. You want close-up detailed pictures of any designs. If there is damage – don't just say it in the description make sure to include one or two pictures of the afflicted area. Let potential buyers decide for themselves how bad the damage is.

eBay lets you upload 12 free pictures with every listing. Include as many as you need to tell your story.

With that said, let's take a closer look at how you can make sure you always have the best pictures available for your eBay listings.

1) **Pay attention to where you take your pictures**. A lot of sellers photograph their items in a messy room where you can see all of the clutter in the background of their picture. Right away that makes buyers question how well the item was taken care of.

Don't do this…

Here's a recent picture posted in an eBay auction. The description was just as bad, "This auction is for a 1955 Topps #50 Jackie Robinson card. This card is in -vg condition."

Other people include photographs that include pictures of several other items they are selling as well. Several book sellers I've purchased from in the past show a whole run of thirty or forty volumes of books from the same series, even though the auction they are listing is for just one book. The result is you're going to confuse a lot of your potential bidders, because you're sending out mixed signals. A lot of people only read the title, and look at the pictures, before they bid. When they don't receive all of the items you showed in the picture, you're setting yourself up to receive negative feedback.

I used to include a scan of the title page to the magazine my articles were from in each of my listings. In each listing I made sure to tell people the illustration was shown to verify date of publication only, it did not come with the actual item I was selling. I did however, give instructions on how they could right click on the item and print a copy if they would like one. I still had unhappy customers, because they didn't take time to read the fine print, so I soon stopped including these pictures in my listings. It made for a lot fewer problems.

2) **Use a light box**. I found one on eBay several years ago for about $50.00. It's basically a frame with a cloth draped on each side, sort of like a tent, and then you have several small flood lights to shine in, to provide you with proper lighting. My light box came with five different colored backdrops so I could vary the background if I chose to. Depending upon the type and size of items you sell, you can find light boxes in a variety of different sizes.

The idea behind using a light box is it allows you to isolate your item, and surround it with nice even lighting. This way you prevent reflections that can keep people from getting a good clear look at your item. It also shows your item against a nice solid background, so it really stands out.

3) **Use natural light if it is available**. Sunlight will normally give you better lighting for your pictures. Just be sure you aren't shooting pictures in the heat of the day, where the light may be too harsh.

4) **Shoot pictures from different angles**. Your item has many different features. Be sure to capture it from as many different angles as you can. This way, potential buyers will be able to see all of the details and features of what you are selling.

Once again you need to put yourself in the buyer's shoes, and really think about what they would want to see. If you're selling an item that lights up don't just show a picture of it, include a picture with it fully lit up. If you are selling a leather billfold with a hand tooled design, show several close-up pictures of the design. A model car should be treated just like a real car, if the doors and hood open up, get pictures of it. If it's a convertible, and the top comes off, include pictures with the top on and off.

5) **Use a tripod**. If your hand shakes even a little it can make for a fuzzy or blurry picture. Tripods are fairly inexpensive, and will help you take better pictures.

6) **Take close-up photos**, especially for smaller items like coins, stamps, or jewelry. Use the macro function on your camera, and shoot the picture as close-up as you can. Try to make it look like the buyer could just reach out and touch your item.

7) **Add a familiar item for contrast on size**. If you're selling a book, it can be a good idea to photograph it next to a ruler to give buyers a sense of what size your item is. Saying 10 inches is one thing, but when you photograph your item next to the ruler it drives the concept home. You can do the same thing if you're selling, buttons, pins, or any kind of jewelry. Photograph the item next to a dime or a quarter, and people will instantly make the size connection.

8) **Don't use flash**. Using flash can cause your pictures to look distorted or blurry.

Finally consider adding video to your auction, especially if you are selling something that easily lends itself to a video presentation.

You don't need anything fancy. If you're selling a radio controlled car or plane, shoot a quick video of someone putting it through its paces. If you are selling woman's fashions, shoot a video of a pretty girl modeling a bathing suit or dress.

Another idea is to shoot a short two or three minute video of you describing your business, how you got started, or talking about something that makes your business unique.

If you're selling Blue Ray DVD players or plasma screen TV's, race on over to YouTube and grab an installation video you can embed into your auction. If one isn't available, consider making your own short video. It will make your offering more unique.

Embedding a YouTube video is as simple as it comes.

1) Upload your video to your YouTube channel

2) Uncheck *show suggested videos when the video finishes*. You don't want to distract your buyers by showing someone else's video. They might just leave your auction all together.

3) Select use *old embed code*

4) Choose the size of video that you want to use

5) Highlight the html code, and paste it into your listing where you want the video to play

Hot to write a good item description

Writing a good eBay item description is a lot like crafting a short story. The more details and personality you put into it, the better the chances are it's going to engage potential buyers, and get them to bid on your item.

The journalist's tool kit includes the questions: Who, what, where, when, why, and how. Answer as many of these questions as you can in each item description, and you will sell more items. Leave any of them out, and people are going to be left with unanswered questions about what you are selling.

Who. Buyers want to know who made the item you're selling. Is it an Apple, Nike, or JVC. If you're selling a book, you need to tell people who the author is. Be sure to give as much information as you can about who made the item, what the brand is, or any other identifying names you find on it. If it's a name most people won't recognize, add a few lines telling them who made it, and why that's important.

What. Tell people exactly what you are selling. While it may be obvious to you, many people aren't going to understand, even if you include plenty of pictures. Your job is to tell people what your item is, and what it does.

Don't just say you have an iPad. Tell them you have "an iPad Mini, and it's great when you're on the go. Just put it in your pocket and you always have internet and all of your contact info close by." If you're selling a book, tell people what the actual title is! I don't know how many books I've seen listed just as an old book about "cowboys, Indians, and cavalry fighting Sitting Bull on the western plains." That's a great combination of keywords, but you still need to say exactly what it is you are selling.

Where. Tell people where your item was made. Is it a Carson City silver dollar, or was it made at the Philadelphia mint. Is it an original Black Forest cuckoo clock, or is it a reproduction clock made in Taiwan. Don't leave people guessing tell them what they need to know.

People also want to know where the item is located. If there are a lot of similar items available on eBay, oftentimes people will choose to purchase items located closer to them, so they can save money on shipping.

When. When was your item made? Is it the most recent model of iPhone, or is it a first generation model. If you're selling collectibles, people want to know when it was made, or if you are unsure, at the very least mention what era it is from.

Here are a few examples:

1) 1950's era Baseball cards
2) Turn of the century sports card memorabilia
3) 1955 Topps Hank Aaron baseball card in near mint condition

Why. Tell people why they need it. "This 1955 Hank Aaron Topps card is one of the keys to completing this vintage set. This one is in near mint condition and can easily be one of the highlights of your collection."

"Golden era comic books are getting harder to find, especially without torn pages or small rips in the spine. Snap this one up now, while you still can."

Give them a compelling reason why they need to buy your item – NOW!

How. Tell potential buyers how the item was made. Was it hand crafted? Made by a colony of elves in the Middle Earth? Or was it made at the Tootsie Roll factory on Cicero Avenue in Chicago?

Tell buyers how you are going to ship their item. Are you shipping by USPS, UPS, or FedEx. If you're selling a delicate collectible like a vintage doll, Hummel figurine, or china set, be sure to tell people how carefully you are going to package their items so there won't be any damage during shipping.

Some items are better suited to telling a good story, than others. Look over the description I wrote for an 1836 copy of the Annals of Congress. I paid $8.00 for it on eBay, and resold it four weeks later for $327.00. The guy I bought it from listed a group of old Government books in fair to average condition. As a result I was able to buy eight of these for $63.00, and sell them for just over $2000.

A lot of times, how much money you make, and how many bidders you get, is determined by how good of a story you can tell.

Here is my description of that book:

This is a really awesome book! It's old, and does have a few problem areas I want to share with you. It was published in 1836. It has a brown leather cover, and as you probably know, leather starts chipping and flaking when it gets to be this age, so you need to be careful, or you will have brown leather all over your hands and clothes. The front cover is detached. I still have it, and it is in really good shape. You can check out the picture, and see for yourself. The spine has some chipping, but it is intact. And the really nice thing is, there is a ribbed area containing the title and date range, and that is all still there too.

And, did I mention, this book is stamped right inside on the first few pages, "Congressional Library." That means this book was in Washington when Abraham Lincoln and Daniel Webster were there. Did they actually page through it? I can't promise you anything, but it's possible.

This book contains some amazing information. It seems there was some trouble brewing down in Texas around this time. Some of the page headers mention – Texas Independence, Conflict in Texas, Movement of Santa Anna's Army, and the Alamo. And, then there are other mentions about canals, roads, Post Office department, and military fortifications.

This is part three of a longer series of books from the Congressional session that year. I'm not sure how many volumes there were altogether.

It's definitely a one of a kind collectible. Feel free to contact me with any questions.

Other times you may just want to play with people's heads, and see if you can make a listing go viral. Consider this one.

Aunt Edna died in the upstairs bedroom over a hundred years ago, but over the years many people in the family have thought she still might be there. Grandma remembers seeing her on the stairs one night when she was a kid. They were having a sleep over, and Edna appeared on the stairs out of nowhere, and then she was gone. Mom and her sisters remember dresser drawers being slammed open and shut with nobody around to do it when they were kids.

Me, I don't remember anything. I was out of town last week, but when I came home dad was going on and on about all of the noise one night in the hall by the little bathroom. No one was upstairs at the time, and it was scaring the bejeezus out of mom, she's 86 now.

He'd read that if you put peanut butter in a Mason jar, sometimes that was a good way to lure ghosts. That night he set out a couple jars with just a dab of peanut butter, and then he waited. The way he tells it, it was just after midnight, he heard the clinking of glass, and he jumped out and slapped the cover on that Mason jar – right quick like.

Caught her, he did, and that's how Aunt Edna came to be in this Mason jar, her ghost that is.

Anyway, we were figuring she's been in our family long enough. This is a great chance for someone else to have her, Mason jar and all. Just be careful not to open the cap. She's probably not going to fall for that same trick twice.

What I am trying to say here is: Don't be afraid to have fun with your item description. You're selling your items to real people, and many of them will enjoy a little humor, as long as you don't forget to include all of the details they need to make an informed decision.

That brings us to my next point. **Full disclosure is not an option**. If you want to continue selling on eBay, you really need to tell people, the good, the bad, and the ugly, about every item you are selling.

Imagine how disappointed you'd be if you ordered a gently used pair of Guess jeans online, and when receive them you discover the stitching is coming undone in some of the seams, and there are faint grass stains on one of the knees. You'd be pissed off, because the seller didn't mention either of those defects in their listing. Maybe they showed pictures, but they weren't clear enough, or focused well enough to call out these issues.

The fact is when you write an item description, it needs to tell all of the great things about the item you are selling, but it also needs to slow things down for a minute, and say hey – this item is great, but you should also know it has a few problems.

A funny thing happens when you start to tell people the item you're selling also has a few problems:

1) Buyers begin to tell themselves, "Hey, I can trust this guy." He's not just trying to bullshit me about how good this thing is, because he's also sharing what's wrong with it.

2) They begin telling themselves maybe the problems you're listing aren't so bad, and maybe, just maybe, they can live with them.

3) People are more likely to bid on your item, because they feel you're being honest with them. This can make your so-so item more desirable than another guys mint item, because his description doesn't talk about flaws, and with any used item,

there's bound to be something wrong with it. Tell people what's wrong with your item, and you will diffuse a lot of their concerns about buying from you.

With that said, you can put a more positive spin on many of the defects your items have.

Here's a great description for a vintage baseball card:

This vintage 1955 Topps Jackie Robinson card has been the highlight of my collection for years. I'm not a sports card expert so keep in mind the things I'm going to tell you are just my opinion. The colors are bright and clear. The top right corner has a small ding to it, nothing major, but you may want to keep that in mind when making your decision on this one. And, as you can tell from the second picture I've included the centering on the reverse side is just a little off. With all of that said it's been a great card for me, and one of the first cards I've shown anyone who has taken time to look at my baseball card collection.

The wife wants to take a vacation this year, so it's got to go. My loss is sure to be your gain. Place your bid today.

Compare that to the typical description.

1955 Topps Jackie Robinson Card. Very Good to Fine condition, with a small bang to upper right corner.

Which one would you bid on? Which one do you think is going to attract more bids, and higher offers? The first one of course. It's the same card, but the way it's described makes it sound special, and more like something you've just got to have.

One more example and we will end our discussion of descriptions.

> *I came across this book several years ago, and everyone I show it to thinks it's one of the coolest things they've ever seen. It's called* **The Emigrant's Guide** *to Iowa, and it says it was published in Davenport, Iowa in 1855. It's a small book, 5" across and about 7" tall, and has 233 pages. Now the condition is not the greatest. The cover is red, and if you check out some of my pictures, you can see the spine is in pretty rough shape. There's a big chunk missing at the top. Other than that it's all held together well, with no loose pages or anything. Inside there is some minor age spotting, but all of the pictures and illustrations are in great shape. I counted seven pictures as I was flipping through this book, one of them is of the Old Capitol in Iowa City, and another is of cows grazing in some western Iowa pastures. If you're interested in Iowa history, or are just looking for some unique piece of Iowa's past, this book could be a good choice for you.*

It's got all of the details you need to know, and it tells a great story about the item to draw you into it. Give this method a shot with some of your listings and see what happens.

How to price your items to sell

Pricing is one of the trickiest parts of selling on eBay or any online site, for that matter.

Price your item too high, and no one will buy it. Price your item too low, and you will be leaving profit on the table. The problem is there is no one hundred percent perfect method for pricing your item right out of the box. Pricing is really more of a process, especially if you are selling multiple copies of an item.

For some items pricing is really easy. Commodity items people buy everyday like foodstuffs, DVD's, books, electronics, all sell in a very close price range. If you step out of the accepted price range for the item, your sales will dry up quicker than you think.

Perhaps the easiest way to price your item is to search eBay to see what similar items have recently sold for. To do this you need to use the advanced search function.

To access the Advanced Search function, go to the top of the eBay page. To the right of the search box you will see the word **Advanced** just after the big blue Search box. Go ahead and click on the word **Advanced**.

Type in the name or description of the item you want to search for. Scroll down a little further where it says search including and check the box by **Completed Listings**. Then click enter. This will return a list of all the ended listing for that item within the past thirty days. Items listed in green are items that have sold.

Once you've done this you will be able to see a list of all completed items on eBay. Non-sold listing will appear for thirty days, sold listings will appear for ninety days. After it returns this list you have the option to narrow your search down even further by clicking on active listings (with bids) or completed listings.

The great thing here is you can see how much items similar to yours have recently sold for on eBay.

By looking through completed listings you can easily find the price range your item has sold in. No more guessing about how to price your items.

The way I use the information is to look through the titles to find items most similar to mine. Each time I click into an item I take a few notes about any keywords the seller used in the title and item description. I also make a note of what price it sold for. If it was an auction item, I mark down the starting price. Next I look at shipping to determine if the seller offered free shipping, or the options and prices they offered for shipping. Another thing you want to note is what category they listed their item in.

After you do this for four or five items you will have some great information about how to write your item description and title. You should also have an excellent idea of what you can expect your item to sell for.

At this point we're almost ready to start pricing your item. Before you stop doing your research I'd suggest tyou also click into two or three of the items that sold for the highest prices. Look over the notes you made, and see if these listings said anything different than the other ones you looked at. Specifically, did they offer a more detailed description? Did they use different keywords in the title? Did they start at a lower price? Did they use a buy-it-now?

Now you need to determine a pricing strategy.

Some people swear by starting everything at 99 cents or $9.99 and letting the market determine the price. The problem with this strategy is it only works for certain categories of items. If you're selling something that always closes in a tight price range like electronics, cell phones, iPhones, iPads, and the like, starting your item at 99 cents is going to bring in the maximum number of bidders, and will normally bring you the highest price possible for each item.

If you're selling one of a kind items collectibles, and other low demand items, starting your item at 99 cents is going to be a disaster. What's going to happen in nine out of ten cases is, if your item sells at all, it's going to sell for 99 cents, or $1.04.

A better pricing strategy with many items is to price them at the lowest price you are willing to accept, and then add a buy-it-now at what you would like to get. If you are selling your item in a fixed price format, set the price somewhat higher than you hope to get, and add best-offer to it.

What if you're selling something unique, that isn't currently available on eBay? How do you price your item then?

If it's something you have a lot of, or a lot of similar items the best thing you can do is experiment with different prices, and determine which one sells the most items.

Let me give you an example. I sell old magazine articles, removed from bound magazines. So basically, all I'm selling is a few sheets of old paper. I have a few competitors on eBay, but not many.

When I first started selling magazine articles back in 2000, I priced all of my items at $12.99, and they sold really well. After about six months I increased my price to $15.99, and then $19.99, and then $25.99, and sales kept increasing each time. When I stretched it again to $27.99, sales started slowing down. As a result, I knew my optimal price range was somewhere between $19.99 and $25.99.

I found my sweet spot in auction pricing the same way. I started my items at $9.99 and many of them sold. Then I added Buy-it-Now at 15.99, $19.99, and $25.99. Once again $25.99 provided the most conversions, so that's the formula I went with – a $9.99 starting price, with a $25.99 Buy-it-Now.

It was a great price strategy and it worked for years.

The next thing you know, eBay decided they wanted to be more like Amazon, and to become more of a market so they could lure in the big sellers like Best Buy and Toy-R-Us.

One of the things they did was to change the emphasis to fixed price listings rather than auctions. That sent me back to the drawing board, and once again, I reinvented my eBay business, this time focusing it around fixed price listings, with a just a scattering of auction listings.

Seller reputation or feedback

The only thing an eBay seller has is his good name or his reputation.

Feedback on eBay is earned each time you complete a successful transaction. If sellers are happy, they have the opportunity to leave feedback. Feedback is based on a five star rating system, plus a one line comment where the seller can say something good or bad about your product or service.

In an ideal world anything above four would be passing, but in eBay's convoluted grading system anything less than a 4.8 average is marginal, and if you fall below a 4.6 average feedback score, you are in danger of losing your buying and selling privileges.

You can check your feedback score at any time by visiting your seller dashboard.

Seller performance numbers		Updated daily
3 months (12/01/12 - 02/28/13) ▾		Transactions: 192 See your reports
Average detailed seller ratings	**Your average**	**Low ratings (1s and 2s)**
Item as described	4.96	0.52% (1)
Communication	5.00	0.00% (0)
Shipping time	5.00	0.00% (0)
Shipping and handling charges	4.96	0.00% (0)
Buyer Protection cases		**Your percentage (count)**
Opened cases		0.00% (0)
Closed cases without seller resolution		0.00% (0)

Performance numbers are from transactions with buyers in the United States.

Using the radio bar you can view your rating for the previous three months, or for the previous twelve months. It gives you your DSR ranking in each category, your percentage of low ratings where you received one or two stars, the number of transactions you completed in the period, and your percentage numbers for buyer protection cases filed.

One area all sellers are susceptible to problems in is shipping and handling fees. Even if you charge fair shipping fees, or subsidize part of the shipping fees, you are always open to customer perceptions. Some customers think five dollars is unfair for shipping a fifty pound computer printer, other buyers will be ok with a five dollar charge for shipping a few pieces of paper. The thing is you never know which type of customer you're going to get.

One way to avoid a negative item strike for shipping fees is to offer free shipping. If you offer free shipping eBay automatically gives you a Five Star rating for the shipping and handling category. So if this is an area you discover is constantly dragging your DSR rating down, you may want to find a way to offer your customers free shipping.

Shipping and handling time is a category where you really have limited control over what happens.

The main thing you can do here is to mail items immediately, or within your promised time frame, and upload tracking information into the system as soon as possible. If you do this every time, you can prove you did everything possible to get the item on its way quickly.

The sad thing is there are still going to be snags.

Sometimes the mailman cannot deliver the item, so he will leave a tag for the customer telling them they need to pick up their package at the post office. The problem is the tag can blow away, or someone else in the house may get the tag, and not show it to your customer. Other times the mailman may mess up and deliver your item to the wrong house. It happens every day. If you provide tracking on all of your items, you can usually figure out what happened, and tell customers exactly where the hold-up is.

Another problem area is international shipping. Nine times out of ten everything goes properly, and your customer will receive their package within seven to ten business days, sometimes much faster. Other times, the item can get caught up in customs, or held up at a post office somewhere along the way, and take six to eight weeks or more to deliver.

The best you can do here is to set realistic expectations. A good way to do this is to let international buyers know up front in your auction description what they can expect in terms of delivery times. I like to say something like this, "All international shipping is by first class mail. Normal delivery time is two to three weeks, but can take as many as six weeks depending upon customs and handling times." This way, when an international customer writes you a few days, or weeks later wondering when they can expect delivery, you can refer them back to your original information. Most customers understand when I use this approach, because the information is not coming at them out of the blue like I am making excuses. Instead, it is just a matter of reinforcing what you already told the customer.

Item as described and communication are all about you.

If you followed the information presented earlier in this guide, and provided an accurate and honest item description, supplemented with several great pictures you should eliminate ninety-nine percent of all items not as described cases.

Take my sales as an example I sell magazine articles and pictures extracted from old magazines. I know from past experience this can cause confusion with some customers because even though I clearly tell them it is a "magazine article carefully extracted from a vintage magazine," I still get emails or feedback saying, "I was expecting a book, and all I got was a page taken out of a book or magazine." The truth is I tell people three times in each item listing exactly what they are buying, and it is not a book or a complete magazine, just an article.

So when I get a bad feedback or a message from a customer demanding a refund I tend to get a little pissed off, but I bite my tongue, and send them the following response.

"I'm sorry you're not happy with the item you purchased. I can understand your frustration I would feel the same way. Here at history-bytes we try our hardest to accurately describe every item that we sell. Each item is carefully labeled within the item description as 'a vintage magazine article carefully extracted from a vintage magazine, not the entire magazine.' If you are unhappy with your item I will be more than happy to take it back and offer you a full refund, shipping included. Keep me advised."

This throws the ball back into the customer's court. I politely tell them what they should already know if they had taken time to read the auction description. At the same time, if they are really unhappy, they know I will take the item back for a full refund. In most cases the customer writes back and tells me even though the item isn't quite what they expected, they are happy with it and will keep it.

Out of thirty thousand sales over the past fourteen years, I've had fewer than ten items returned, so I can guarantee you this method will work for you.

You're also going to receive frivolous complaints from customers hoping to shame you into giving them a discount. I've probably had at least a hundred people email to tell me the item I sent them was incomplete and either some pages or pictures were missing. Again, I know the odds of that are unlikely, because I packaged and mailed the item myself. I follow the same path with these customers that I do with other customer service issues, I apologize, and I offer a full refund.

Once again, because I don't take the offensive or get mad, most of the customers tell me it's OK, and they want to keep the item anyway, even though it is incomplete. Odds are they were just shooting for a discount, otherwise they would have returned the item if it really was incomplete.

That brings us back to communication. Ninety-five percent of your customers don't require any special communication. As long as their item is mailed on time and you promptly upload tracking information your customer is going to give you the five stars.

The other five percent of your customers are going to have questions before or after the sale. As long as you get back to them within twenty-four hours and give them a friendly response, you will be ok. It's when you blow them off, and don't bother to respond to repeated requests for more information you're going to have trouble.

You need to know your numbers

*(This section is from my book **Sell It Online**. Bookkeeping is one of those things that confuse both new and experienced sellers. It's important to track your sales, know your numbers, and report your sales properly for tax purposes. Keep in mind – this section is just an overview of accounting for eBay sellers - it is not a substitute for talking with your accountant or tax professional.)*

The absolute worst thing that can happen is you go full blast into online selling thinking you're making beau-coups bucks because money keeps pouring into your PayPal account, only to discover it isn't so. Unfortunately this happens way too often.

To make a profit in any business, you need to know your numbers.

There is a huge difference between money coming in, and making a profit. To make a profit you need to make enough money to cover all of your expenses, plus the cost of the items you are selling. Anything left over after covering all of your expenses is your profit.

Sounds easy, doesn't it?

Here are just a few of the expenses you're going to have in any online venture:

1) Cost of the goods you are selling

2) eBay fees (Store fee, listing fees, final value fees, extras)

3) Internet fees

4) PayPal or merchant account processing fees

5) Packing supplies (boxes, envelopes, peanuts, bubble wrap)

6) Postage (insurance, shipping, tracking fees)

7) Collateral services (Auctiva, Vendio, Ink Frog – any similar tools you use to enhance listings or for picture storage)

8) Advertising (Google or Amazon pay per click ads)

9) Automobile expenses (gas, mileage – for going to post office, shopping for supplies, or purchasing inventory)

10) Phone, fax, computer, scanner, digital camera

11) Home office expenses (desk, chair, and expenses for remodeling your office)

12) Home related bills (if you choose to claim the home office deduction, you can also deduct the portion of utilities, sewer, trash and other home related expenses)

The fact is, all of these expenses add up quickly, and if you don't keep careful track of them, you can easily fool yourself into thinking you're making a profit, when the truth of the matter is, you're losing your ass.

One of the better tools available for tracking your income and expenses is Outright. Outright (now known as GoDaddy Bookkeeping) is a computer app, available to all sellers in your **My eBay** tab. Click where it says **Applications** at the top of the page, and you can search for Outright.

Outright is free to install and use for the basic version. There is also a paid version that unlocks additional tools to make your life easier come tax time.

The best thing about Outright is it runs within eBay, so every time you visit eBay, you can check out where you are profit wise for the month. Another great thing about using Outright is it works across multiple marketplaces, so you can collect all of your sales and expense information in one place.

Outright integrates with eBay, Amazon, Etsy, and numerous online stores. Every day it automatically goes into each of your accounts and updates your sales and expenses. You can also add your business checking accounts or credit cards, and it will automatically import information from them.

A separate tab allows you to record mileage. You have the ability to manually add income or expenses from other sources, so you have total control over your business accounts.

Probably the best thing about using Outright is most of the work is done for you automatically. This keeps you from forgetting to record expenses you might otherwise miss.

You can also train it to recognize certain expenses, so it will automatically record them to a specific account from then on. An example here is Stamps.com. I have it connected to my postage expense account, and every time it comes across a Stamps.com charge on my PayPal account, it records the charge to my postage expense account.

Other sellers opt to record expenses in Excel or Quick Books. The main thing is: You need to save all of your receipts, and keep a record of all of your sales and expenses.

At the end of the year, you are required to report all of your online income on your tax forms.

To keep everyone honest, the government has imposed mandatory reporting requirements upon PayPal. If more than $20,000 is deposited into your PayPal account during the course of the year, PayPal is required to report it to the IRS on form 1099-K.

To view your form 1099-K sign into your PayPal Account, hover your pointer over the **history** tab, and this will bring up a drop down menu. You want to click on **tax documents**, and this will give you the option to view a PDF file of your 1099-K, if one was generated for you.

At this time you are not required to submit the PayPal 1099-K with your income tax filing, but you should be sure that you are reporting at least as much income as is shown on it. You can be sure that the IRS is matching them up, and taking a close look at your 1099-K, and the income you report on your tax return.

Selling beyond eBay

It took me nearly five years to try selling off of eBay. My first attempt was a Yahoo storefront. It was easy to setup, and in about three months I had nearly 5,000 items listed there. The only problem was I didn't have any sales. Not a single one.

Even though I was a success on eBay, and had over six hundred buyers every month, I had no effective way to drive those customers to my own website. Today I have an Amazon web store, and I still have difficulties driving traffic to it.

Having your own website is a great strategy if you have a strong following, or a great plan for helping people to find you there. Barring that I would suggest looking at other market places to expand to.

Many of the market places make it extremely easy for eBay sellers to make the transition to them.

Many of these markets also offer very limited sales compared with selling on eBay. So before you get all excited about saving fees, test the waters first, and find out which markets will actually work for you, and allow you to make adequate sales.

eCRATER is one site that I've had fairly good luck with. They have a wizard that will automatically import all of your eBay items, including some of your eBay feedback so you don't have to start out from scratch.

The good thing about eCRATER is: There are absolutely no fees for listing or selling your items. You get to keep 100% of your sales. The bad thing about eCRATER is: Compared to selling on eBay, you're going to make a lot fewer sales.

All told I make twelve to fifteen sales per year on eCRATER despite the fact I have over 6000 items listed there, so it's good for a twenty or twenty-five bucks a month. The only reason I stay there is I don't have to do anything but update my inventory by synching it with eBay occasionally.

bidStart is another site that's easy to get started on. Like eCRATER they make it real easy to import your entire inventory with a couple clicks of a button. For an extra ten bucks every month they will automatically synch your inventory so it's always up to date.

Again traffic is limited. I've made seven or eight sales here in the last year. They do charge final value fees, but nothing for listing or importing your items, unless you decide to add their synching services with eBay.

Etsy is a great site for crafters according to everything I've heard. Fees appear to be quite reasonable, just 20 cents to list an item for four months, and a 3.5 percent final value fee. Most of the items on the site are handmade crafts or crafting supplies, although they do allow limited vintage items over twenty years old as well.

Amazon does offer several good Kindle books about selling on Etsy.

- Selling on Etsy: Turning Your Hobby Into A Profitable Business, by Megan Kutchman.
- Etsy Selling Success: Cash in on Your Creations, by Elyse Reynolds.
- Etsy-preneurship: Everything You Need to Know to Turn Your Hand Made Hobby Into a Thriving Business, by Jason Malinak.
- Etsy 101: Sell Your Crafts on Etsy, the DIY Marketplace for Handmade, Vintage and Crafting Supplies, by Steve Weber.

eBid. eBid has been touted by several sites and surveys as a strong challenger to eBay. It's never worked well for me. I tried eBid because for a onetime $49.00 fee, you can sell free for life, with no additional fees, period. The problem is in three years listing items on the site, I've only made one sale.

The other major problem I see for eBay sellers wanting to make the transition to eBid is they don't offer an easy way to move your items to the site. Sellers have to download a spreadsheet, load their eBay items into it, and then upload the items back to eBid.

My thought on this one is: Don't waste your time. Wait until they get more traffic, and develop a simple interface to move your eBay store items.

Ruby Lane. Like Etsy, I don't have any personal experience with this one. Their fee structure is somewhat different. They charge a $20 per month fee, a 30 cent listing fee for each item, and another monthly fee based upon the number of items you sell each month.

I've heard good and bad things about Ruby Lane. It is another alternative to eBay that has worked for some sellers.

Bonanza. This is another site I've had items listed on for just over three years, with basically no luck. I've sold three items in all of that time, and had a few buyers offer me one half or one third of my asking price.

The good news about Bonanza is it's free to list your items, and they have a great interface for importing your items. The bad news is they have no traffic.

I saved the best option for last, and that of course is Amazon.com.

I've been selling on Amazon for almost a year and a half now, and outside of eBay, Amazon has given me the best bang for my buck.

I consistently sell thirty to forty items per month. I don't have to worry about receiving best offers, or people complaining the shipping charge is too high.

More importantly, I actually make money using Amazon. Most months I clear $500 to $700 after fees, and a few months it has jumped up over $1000.

The rules of the game are a little different on Amazon than they are on eBay, and I admit I still haven't got them all figured out, but I'm making money all along the way as I learn.

I first tried selling on Amazon five or six years ago, and sold maybe five or ten items a year, but I only had about four hundred items listed there at that time.

About a year and a half ago I came across a company called **Export Your Store**.

The great thing about using Export Your Store is they do all of the work for you as far as moving your items from eBay to Amazon. The bad thing about using Export Your Store is Amazon is really nothing like eBay, so after they transfer your items to Amazon you still have a lot of work to do to ensure everything is optimized for Amazon selling.

Here are just a few of the differences between eBay and Amazon that can cause you problems.

. Amazon is a market place. They don't allow personal branding or html code in any of their item description pages.

. Amazon doesn't allow any references to your business in their description pages.

. Amazon requires tags (keywords) to be entered in the proper section of their listing form to help buyers find your item in search.

The folks at Export Your Store are really good at stripping out all of the html code in your listings, and getting them moved over. I had ten thousand items exported from eBay to Amazon in just over two days.

Then I started receiving a slew of item violation warnings from Amazon. At the time I did this you could still have your customer service email address in your eBay listings. This violated Amazon's terms of service, and I was forced to go through just over 10,000 items, one at a time, and edit each of them individually.

I went through three weeks of hell, spending twelve to fourteen hours of every day, checking, revising, and deleting listings.

A few other things I discovered while editing my listings was sometimes when they stripped out the html code from my listing templates, they also removed part of my item descriptions including the SKU numbers I used to locate items once they were sold. I also had to add keywords to every single Amazon listing (I think this was because I sell one of a kind collectibles and each item required adding a new page to the Amazon catalog). If you're selling more traditional items, like electronics, books, CD's, or DVD's that already have a catalog page, this would probably not be an issue.

With all the problems I mentioned, I would still recommend Export Your Store. Customer service was responsive, and they worked quickly. The current charges for exporting your eBay store to Amazon are $299. They will also synch your new and sold items for $99 per month.

Other companies are also available to perform the export for you. Among them are Vendio and Linnworks.

Or, if you are more daring, Amazon does allow you to FTP your items.

Top 10 tools to help you sell on eBay

eBay information

1) **eCommerce Bytes**. If you're an online seller you need to read this to keep up with what's going on. Ecommerce Bytes blog will keep you informed about what's happening in the world of online sales. Sign up for their daily email updates, and take a few minutes every day to read a few articles. They're short, and informative.

2) **Channel Advisor Blog**. This one contains a lot of information and reports about selling on eBay, strategies you can use, and is more detailed than ecommerce bytes.

3) **The Online Seller**. Although this e-zine is provided by Auctiva, it gives a lot of great info about how to sell on eBay and other ecommerce sites. Some recent stories include – Selling on eBay as an eBay Consignment Specialist, Online Auction Sites Other Than eBay, and Is Selling on Etsy Right for You? (a multi-part series). Most of the articles are short, easy to read, and will get you thinking of ways to help grow your eBay business.

Picture Hosting & Auction Hosting Services

4) **Auctiva** is the largest auction hosting and picture hosting service. Fees range up to $40 per month depending on the number of pictures being hosted. The major disadvantage with Auctiva is they are eBay specific, and do not integrate with Amazon like some of the other services do.

5) **Vendio** allows sellers to list and synch items on eBay and Amazon. Fees range from $24.95 to $149.95 depending upon your monthly dollar volume of sales, and the number of items you have for sale.

6) **Ink Frog** is an eBay specific auction and picture hosting service.

7) **Channel Advisor** is a multi-channel ecommerce platform that allows you to sell on eBay, Amazon, Buy.com, Sears, and Newegg. They also can help with Social Media, paid search advertising, and planning selling strategies.

Mailing services

8) **Stamps.com** is run by the United States Post Office and can help sellers mail their products more efficiently. Using Stamps.com sellers can import buyer information from eBay, Amazon, Etsy, and other marketplaces and print shipping labels on their home computers. Stamps.com will also print International mailing labels and customs forms. There are two levels of service: a free version for eBay sellers and a basic version for $15.99.

9) **Endicia** offers a number of mailing services similar to Stamps.com. Their monthly fees start at $9.99. They also allow sellers to add a logo to their labels to help promote their brand.

Multi-Channel selling

10) **Export Your Store** is a service that helps sellers to easily move their eBay store to the Amazon Marketplace. They offer synching services to keep your eBay and Amazon stores up to date. The cost is $299 for the initial import (they will work with

you on pricing for smaller stores), and $99 per month to synch your items.

Top 10 Tips to help grow your eBay business

1) **Build your brand**. Don't just make sales take time to build your brand. People don't just buy Apple computers, iPhones, and iPads, they swear by them. They tell their friends about them. People write glowing reviews about items they like, and some of them even hit the Facebook like button.

What I'm trying to say here, is make your business likeable. Be the business people want to tell their friends about. When I first started out, I included a handwritten thank-you note with every item I sold. As my business got bigger, this got harder to do. One thing I did was to print up blank Thank-you cards with Vista Print. Whenever I make a large sale, I write a personalized note on one of these and include it when I mail their items.

Sometimes for no reason at all, I will send some of these cards out to some of my better buyers. When I do this I don't try to sell them anything. I just say "it was great doing business with you. I hope you're enjoying all of your items. Have a great day, Nick."

I also built a website, digitalhistoryproject.com that I share with people who purchase from me. From time to time I will post articles and pictures on it that I think my customers would enjoy. It's entirely free. They don't have to buy anything. But when they go there, it has links to my eBay and Amazon stores, and to some of my Kindle Books.

The website gives people one more way to connect with me, without my having to try and sell to them.

Build your brand to keep your customers coming back to you.

2) **Experiment with new products**. No one can make money selling the same products forever. People change. Their needs change. You need to change along with your customers, and be one step ahead of them, so you can have the products they want there and waiting for them when they are ready.

Don't be afraid to try new items. What's the worst that can happen? They won't sell. If this happens, forget about it, and move on to your next product.

No one hits a home run every time they're up to bat. You don't have to either. Just keep looking for new products, and you will find yourself coming up with more winners than losers.

If you have any doubt about this strategy, look at Mountain Dew or Frito Lay. Every month they bring out a new version of their product. Ninety-nine percent of them disappear, but the winners stick around, and help them enjoy increased sales.

Do the same thing to help grow your business.

3) **Automate everything you can**. Life is easier when you put things on autopilot.

When I first started, I used to leave all of my feedback myself. Once I started selling 500 items per month, leaving that much feedback became a burden, and I automated it. Now I never have to worry about feedback. As soon as a customer makes their payment with PayPal, the system leaves feedback for me.

The same goes with my eBay listings. I always use *good till cancelled* for my fixed price listings. That way I never have to do anything. They are always running. My auctions style listings are set up the same way. I set them to automatically relist a certain number of times if they don't sell. This way I don't need to do anything until they either sell or quit being relisted.

If you want more time to run your business, or if you want to have more free time to spend with your family, put as many tasks as you can on autopilot.

4) **Price doesn't matter**. Contrary to what you think, you don't have to have the lowest price. Don't be afraid to be the highest priced seller. Often time's price is only one of many factors that influence customers to buy from you.

Like any eBay seller, I have competitors, but I've always tried to set myself apart from the competition. To do this I offer a wide variety of items, tell an intriguing story where needed, offer quick shipping and responsive customer service.

My thought is I offer a great product that people enjoy, why shouldn't I charge a premium price?

Another component to this is many people perceive that a higher priced item is more valuable. It is true there are always two or three other sellers on eBay who sell the same items I do, some of them at half the price, but a lot of sellers choose to buy from me anyway.

Why? Part of it is I've got great feedback. I also have one of the largest selections of vintage magazine articles available on eBay, and have had for the last fourteen years. Because of this many of the customers who bought from me when I first started selling online, are still with me today. And, even when the economy is slow, I can count on making sales to them.

5) **Free shipping may not be the answer**. Don't let eBay bully you into offering free shipping. If you're thinking about offering free shipping, test, and test some more, to make sure it actually makes sense for you, and brings in more sales.

eBay has done a lot of studies that show customers like free shipping. They also know from customer feedback shipping charges are one of the largest trouble areas on the site. Even if seller's charge fair shipping, or offer discounted shipping, a lot of buyers think what you charge them is unfair.

My suggestion is: Make sure free shipping is actually going to work for you, before you roll it across all of your items.

I've tried offering free shipping several times, and it's never worked for me. Sales don't magically increase just because you are offering free shipping. You can try rolling all of the shipping costs, or a portion of them into your selling price, but a lot of times, that just decreases yours sales. Buyers are smart enough to understand what you're doing.

My thought is most buyers understand someone has to pay shipping, and as long as they don't feel you're out to make a buck on it, they're going to buy from you.

If you're worried customers are going to balk at your shipping costs, tell people why you charge more. Do you sell delicate items in need of special care and packing? Explain how carefully you pack each item to ensure it will arrive safely. Better yet, shoot a video showing how carefully you pack your items, and include it in every auction.

It's an old sales trick. Answer objections before they come up, and you will sell more items, every time.

6) **Have fun with what you do**. If you enjoy what you're doing, people are going to know. They will see it in the way you word your auction descriptions, and the way you respond in your customer service emails. Too many people come off as assholes in their auction descriptions. They have all of these policies, and list all sorts of warnings. You know the ones I'm talking about, they say —

- You're bid is a legally binding contract
- If you don't like our terms, don't bid
- Returns will not be accepted…

- All items are sold "as is." Read the item description carefully, and make sure this is what you want, before bidding...

I can't think of the last time I bought an item from anybody who puts things like this in their product descriptions, even when I really wanted the item they were selling. Life's too short to deal with those types of people.

Lighten up!

7) **Sell for a cause**. If you want to make your items more visible on eBay, try listing your items in a charity auction.

eBay Giving Works lets sellers donate from 10% to 100% of the selling price of the items they sell to one of the charities listed with them. There are thousands of charities to choose from, and if you've never sold through eBay Giving Works before, one of the great things is: they don't just partner with the large national organizations like the American Red Cross and The United Way. There are also thousands of smaller regional charities you can sell for.

I live in Davenport, Iowa. When I search Giving Works by location to find charities in my city, twelve organizations are listed.

. Disability Assistance Dogs
. K-9 Kindness Rescue, Inc.
. Humane Society of Scott County
. Quad Cities Affiliate of Susan G Komen for the Cure
. United Way of the Quad Cities

. Habitat for Humanity
. Storytellers International
. Adventure Christian Community Church of the Quad Cities
. Gateway Redevelopment Group
. Genesis Health Services Foundation
. King's Harvest
. St. Ambrose University Children's Campus

If I stretch my search out to within ten miles of Davenport, there are over twenty-five local charities I can sell for.

eBay makes it easy to sell for a charity. Just check the box while you're listing your item for sale, and choose what percentage of the sale you would like to donate. eBay also helps out with your fees by crediting a percentage of them back to you.

Whenever I use charity auctions, my page views skyrocket. Normally page views increase two hundred to three hundred percent, especially when I partner with a larger charity.

Try a charity auction next time you sell on eBay. You will sell more items, and you will feel good about yourself.

8) **Don't waste time going to the Post Office**. There are a lot of services out there to help you ship your items. Use them to save time and money on shipping.

You can easily print all of your postage through eBay or PayPal. Just choose the *Print Shipping Label* option.

Two other options are Stamps.com and Endicia. Both of these services charge monthly fees, but they give you more shipping options.

I use Stamps.com, and have for over ten years. There is a $15.99 monthly fee, but it keeps me from having to go inside the Post Office three or four time a week, so it's worth the money to me. The great thing is by using Stamps.com I can mail international items by first class. If I mail the same item using PayPal or eBay, the only shipping options are Priority and Express mail, and those services are way too expensive an option for me to offer to my customers.

Another benefit of using Stamps.com is it allows you to ship all of your items from different marketplaces through one dashboard. Stamps.com lets you add multiple eBay stores, your Amazon store, and your Etsy store, so you can mail everything from one location. It's a whole lot quicker to use, and if you need to provide tracking information, it's available in one place.

Whichever service you choose, it will save you time and money on shipping.

9) **Know your Numbers**. A lot of eBay sellers have no idea how much money they're making or not making. They just assume because money keeps flowing into their PayPal account things are good.

To make a profit on eBay you need to know your numbers. Just about everything you do on eBay has fees associated with it, and if you aren't careful, they can get the better of you – Fast!

Here are just a few of the fees and expenses you need to keep an eye on –

. eBay store fees
. Final value fees
. Auction extras (bold, highlight, picture packs, etc)
. Shipping
. Packing supplies
. Insurance fees
. Picture hosting
. Service providers like Auctiva, Vendio, and Ink Frog
. Actual costs of the item you are selling
. Refunds for lost and disputed items
. Bookkeeping (whether you use an accountant, or an online service like Outright)
. Gasoline
. Wear and tear on your car whenever you go to the Post Office or out to source items or purchase mailing supplies
. Computers, scanners, digital cameras, scales
. Broadband internet access
. Your time

The fact is everything you do on eBay costs money. To make a profit selling on eBay, you need to understand what it really costs you to sell an item.

If you pay five dollars for the item you are selling, and it sells for ten dollars, that gives you a fifty percent profit. Or does it?

eBay fees are going to set you back at least $1.05. PayPal is going to take another .50 to process your transaction. If you have an eBay store, or use a service like Auctiva, you may easily have another $1.00 into your auction. That brings your cost up to $7.55. So now you're at a $2.45 profit. If you offered free shipping, that's another $2.50 to $6.00 depending upon the item you are selling, and how you ship it. Now you're losing money!

At the end of the day, it's really easy to lose money selling on eBay. **If you don't know your numbers you can easily fool yourself into thinking you're making money.**

Know your numbers, and what it's going to take to make a profit.

One other cost most people don't figure in is the cost of your time. If you spend ten hours a week selling on eBay, and only make $25.00, that's $2.50 per hour. Only you can decide how much your time is worth.

10) **Make time for yourself**. Selling on eBay can be a great business, but it can soon become your personal prison, sucking you into working endless hours.

Most eBay sellers work at home. As a result, it's often hard to separate your personal life and your business life.

There's always one more item you can list for sale. You will find yourself constantly checking for emails, and answering customer inquiries at all hours of the day and night. And, there's always sales. You're going to find yourself checking them way too many times, especially when sales are a little slow.

As Detective Adrian Monk would say, "It's a blessing, and a curse."

Unless you want to hate selling on eBay, find a way to shut it off, and make time for yourself. Decide on a cut off time, and stick to it. No eBay after 5:00 pm; or no eBay on weekends.

Make time for yourself.

Top 5 reasons you need to sell off of eBay

1) **Reach more customers**. While it's true eBay does have more buyers than all of the alternatives (except Amazon), the fact is you need to do whatever it takes to attract new buyers.

2) **Many buyers are fed up with eBay**. Over the years eBay has alienated a lot of buyers and sellers, with their constant changes, and site revisions. "Best Match" became "no thanks" as it often times made it harder for buyers to find the items they were looking for. Other people didn't like being told they couldn't pay with check, cash, or money order.

3) **Nothing lasts forever**. As good as eBay is, and as long as they've been the big kid on the block, sooner or later, some new guy is going to come along and push them aside. Remember F.W. Woolworths, Circuit City, or look at what's happening to Blockbuster. Make sure you have a Plan B, just in case.

4) **You will never know until you try**. It's easy to say those eBay alternative sites don't work, but you will never know if they work for you or not, unless you try.

5) **A dollar is a dollar, no matter where you make it**. If you try a new site and you only make one sale a month, that's still money you didn't have.

Seller Profiles

Over the years I've had the opportunity to work with and talk to hundreds of eBay sellers. Some of them were brand new to eBay others have been selling for ten years or more now.

Every one of them has a unique story about how they got started selling on eBay, and about what they expect to take away from it.

Many people I know embraced eBay because it gave them a real opportunity to start their own businesses with little or no risk, other than the time they invested.

A lot of parents have looked at eBay as a chance to stay home with their children and be with them as they are growing up.

For others, eBay has supplemented a lifetime of low wage jobs, or has given them hope after being laid off from a lifetime career in corporate America.

Others have used their eBay incomes as a stepping stone to other careers. Many have become consultants or experts in the product lines they started selling on eBay. Some have become instructors helping other people to start and operate successful online businesses.

For me, eBay gave me extra money to buy new cars and a bigger house when I was working. After a corporate layoff in 2004, selling on eBay gave me the opportunity to build a strong and solid business of my own. Over the last year eBay has become my stepping stone to a new career in writing, and helping other people learn how to start selling on eBay.

The following section profiles a number of eBay sellers I have known, and the businesses they are running on eBay. I look forward to adding you to the list of eBay successes in the not so distant future.

Good luck and great selling!

My eBay story

(This is the bio I included in my first book Freaking Idiot's Guide to Selling on eBay, How anyone can make $100 or more everyday selling on eBay. I thought it might be helpful for everyone to read it over and see how I got started. Maybe it will give you some ideas.)

My own story is typical of many eBay sellers.

I got my first taste of on line auctions in 1999. I had been following eBay and Yahoo Auctions for some time, and one day, I decided to take the plunge. I bought a couple baseball cards.

And then I bought some more, and some more. It was like an addiction.

Anyway, one thing led to another, and pretty soon I had this crazy idea maybe I could sell some baseball cards, too. At this time I was buying "lots" of 1954 and 1955 Topps baseball cards thinking I could piece together a set. Many of the cards were lower grade, with creases and bruised corners, but they were a start.

Whenever I got a better card it went in my set. The other cards ended up in a cast off pile. As time went by I found myself with quite a few of these castoffs. And, they ended up being my first foray into auction selling.

My auctions were pretty unsophisticated at that time. Basically, I would scan a picture of the card, front and back, add a little description, and post it on eBay. Most of them I priced between $1.00 and $5.00 based on how mangled they were.

But the thing is - people bought them. Sometimes I even had bidding wars erupt, where they would jump from $1.00 to $10.00 and even $20.00 occasionally. Pretty cool stuff.

This went on for probably six months, and I was doing ok. I wasn't really making any money, because even though I was selling several hundred dollars-worth of cards a month, I was buying just as much or more. But it felt really good, because people were sending me money. Every day I received cash and checks in the mail, and dutifully I would package those baseball cards up, stuff them in an envelope, and mail them off to their new owners.

It was definitely fun. And to make it more interesting, back in those days, many people sent you cash, so many times, I had ten and twenty dollar bills falling out of all those envelopes.

Then one day I had one of those epiphany moments. I was perusing through the auction listings and caught sight of a guy selling an old magazine article (not a whole magazine, just one article taken from a magazine). It made me stop. And think. What kind of a nutcase would buy, or sell, a magazine article?

I read his description. I looked at his pictures. He was asking $10.00.

I needed to know a little more. So I looked at the other items he was selling, and he had about fifteen or twenty of these magazine articles for sale. Some of them had bids. A couple of them were over $20.00.

I looked at his sold history. And, over the past six months he had sold nearly one hundred magazine articles. Not bad for a few pieces of paper torn out of a musty old book.

I went back to selling my baseball cards. But over the next few weeks my thoughts kept wandering back to that guy selling magazine articles. I liked history. I liked books. It seemed like something I could do.

My first step into this new venture was to purchase a copy of Harper's Magazine from 1865. It had a good mix of articles. Some articles were on the Civil War and others on historical places and events.

My investment was a whopping $15.00. And, like just about all of the items I sell, I bought it on eBay.

When my issue of Harper's arrived I paged through it. Before I took it apart, I made a list of which articles I was going to sell, how I was going to describe them, and how much I was going to ask for them.

Anyway, to make a long story short, I sold most of those articles pretty quickly. My $15.00 investment quickly turned into $250.00. And like my venture with baseball cards, I found myself buying more and more, and still more books to break apart and sell.

Today I have over 6,000 items listed on eBay, and just over 10,000 on Amazon.

Over the past thirteen years I have completed nearly 30,000 sales as history-bytes on eBay alone. I'm just ending my first year of selling on Amazon, and have racked up close to 200 sales there. It's proving to be a tough nut to crack compared to eBay, but I will make it happen.

After being laid off in 2004, I jumped into eBay full time. I went from making $500 a month to $5000 a month.

Before doing this, I read everything written about eBay that I could get my hands on. I had someone design a custom template and eBay store interface for me. I plugged my picture into every auction listing hoping to build trust into my listings. I offered a "100% Money Back Guarantee – No Questions Asked."

I went from having 500 listings in my eBay store to maintaining almost 10,000 items listed for sale at any given time. I was listing 400 items each and every week, and I was mailing out nearly 150 packages every week.

It was more work than having a job. I don't think there was a single week that I clocked under 70 hours. It was a seven day work week.

And this is pretty much true of every full time eBay seller I have ever talked with or read about. It's a 24 / 7 job.

You get hooked on it.

Many of my best sales came about by accident. Others happened because of deliberate planning, and a whole lot of luck.

In growing my business I took a lot of chances.

I stretched the barrier every chance I could on pricing. Many of the sellers in my category were selling the same items I was selling for a whole lot less. I was asking $25.00 or $30.00, they were asking $5.00 or $10.00 for the same thing. I decided long ago to go for the gusto. My items have always sold better at a higher price.

I found myself trying a lot of new things.

One of my great successes was selling newspapers. I bought every bound volume I could of the Niles Weekly Register. It was one of the first real National newspapers in America. Over time I was able to assemble almost a complete run from 1811 to 1833.

From 1812 to 1815 they contained great accounts of battles and leaders in the War of 1812. I read through every paper, and listed them on eBay one by one. I included excerpts of battlefield accounts in all of my listings. Two of them on the burning of the White House went for about $100 each. Another, from 1811, contained a printing of the Declaration of Independence, side-by-side with Jefferson's notes for it. That one garnered $250.

I even tried bundling with a few of them. Two of our presidents, Thomas Jefferson and John Adams, died on July 4, 1826. Four papers were dedicated to their lives, an account of their deaths, and news of their funerals. These papers sparked some of the hottest bidding any of my auctions ever received. The final price they sold for was over $500.

Another time I was bidding on an 1840's copy of George Catlin's **Letters and Notes**. I lost the bid. It sold for over $500. But another seller emailed me she had a copy she was willing to part with for $200. I jumped on it, and sold the individual pictures for over $3500. It was a nice score, and brought me lots of new customers.

I stumbled across eight bound volumes of the **Annals of Congress** from the 1830's for $10 each. They were filled with news of the battle at the Alamo and Mexican troop movements in Texas. The Mormon exodus from Illinois and Missouri was discussed over and over again, along with many other popular topics of the day. Once again, I was able to sell individual pages about the Alamo and the Mormon's for $100 or more – each.

If I could tell sellers anything about eBay, it would be to develop a specialty that no one else is serving, and work it for all its worth.

Many of my customers have been with me since the first days I started selling on eBay. They know I'm always out there searching for new and unique things. And they appreciate that, and keep coming back to see what new articles I've discovered.

Over the years I've sold items to: the White House Historical Society, the Royal Museum in Jamaica, castles and historical societies all over the United States, Europe, Japan, China, Russia, Australia, and more. Hundreds of authors and publishers count on me for information when they are writing books, and illustrating magazine articles and books.

Museums buy illustrations and articles every day to augment their displays.

Probably the most off the wall sale I ever made was an article I found in a 1950's movie star magazine. There was a letter a from a pregnant movie star to her unborn daughter. Fifty years later her daughter saw that article in one of my listings, and purchased a letter from her mom that she had never seen, or even knew existed.

In the thirteen years that I've been selling on eBay technology has changed. People's wants and needs have changed. I now have my own website, digitalhistoryproject.com. I'm offering many of my more popular magazine articles as Kindle and Nook Books.

If you would like to see my eBay store, you can visit history-bytes.

Who knows where your eBay journey will take you?

John - Sports cards

John began collecting sports cards as a kid. He got his start selling them in the early 1990's when he was still in college. After school the card market softened, and the show circuit sort of fell apart, so he socked all of his cards away. Once or twice a year he would do a few card shows just to keep his hat in the game, but most times he was lucky if he sold enough cards to pay his table fees.

In 2001 a friend introduced John to Yahoo auctions, and he caught the selling bug all over again. In the beginning he would list ten or twenty cards per week, and normally sell twelve or thirteen of them.

One thing he noticed was online buyers weren't as worried about condition, as people at shows. In fact many of his Yahoo buyers were voracious buyers of filler cards (cards in fair to poor condition).

To keep up with the demand he started buying "lots" of cards, or near complete sets, and breaking them up. Often times, he could sell the individual cards for $3.00 to $5.00 each, and if he was lucky there were a few cards in better condition that he could get $10.00 or $20.00 for.

Up to this point he was selling cards from his own collection, and supplementing them with collections he would buy on line.

In 2002 he moved the majority of his business to eBay. Once there he found the buyers were more reliable, and more likely to pay for the items they bid on. Yahoo was littered with a lot of dead beat buyers, and often times it was a crapshoot waiting to see if they would pay or not.

The move to eBay exposed John to a larger audience, and he began to sell more cards than ever before. One of the challenges now was getting enough cards to keep his sales growing. To meet the demand he started going to bigger card shows, and setting up tables just to buy cards, not to sell. He spent more time scouring eBay listings to grab any "lot" he thought gave him the potential to break up, and sell the cards individually.

The strategy worked great. According to John he "was working seventy even eighty hours a week just to keep up" with the demand. His fiancé even jumped in and helped with the mailing. Many times they were mailing fifty to sixty packages per day.

In early 2008 John started selling high end sports memorabilia – autographs, jerseys, and gloves. By the middle of the year business was really taking off, and John was borrowing more and more money to source better material.

September of that year things started taking a wrong turn. The government announced we were in a recession. By mid-October sales were down twenty-five percent and John was starting to feel the hurt.

By January his sales were down fifty-one percent and he was having trouble meeting his loan payments. To make matters worse John's first response was to cut prices. Many times he was barely making a profit, or even losing money after covering his eBay fees.

2009 was a roller coaster ride of declining sales, price cutting, and fending off the bankers as John tried to restructure his eBay business.

No matter what he tried nothing seemed to work. Customers didn't respond to drastically lower prices, and when he tried to package lots to sell excess inventory to other dealers none of them showed any interest either. Many of the other sports memorabilia dealers were feeling the hurt too.

John saw a lot of his competitors disappearing from eBay and was pretty sure he would be suffering the same fate soon.

Finally out of desperation, he partnered with a large eBay consultant who helped him rebrand his business. One of the first things they did was to design a new logo and build a new eBay store with a fancier listing template.

John had an anchor store, but never really used any of its features. His designer quickly changed all of that.

They used the custom pages to build John's brand, and tell people more about the items he sold. The consultant designed individual pages for sports cards, autographs, jerseys, bats, and gloves. The custom pages featured large pictures of items from each category, and talked about how to put each type of collection together, how to take care of your items, and what to look out for when shopping so that you didn't get burned by fakes.

The consultants also showed John how to optimize his gallery pictures to help draw potential bidders into his auctions. Every picture was a close-up, and taken with proper lighting.

They added more pictures to each listing, and made sure buyers could see a potential purchase from every angle.

John's storefront got a more colorful design, and the landing page had category pages buyers could click on to enter the individual listings.

Everything looked professional.

At the same time, John was encouraged to change his inventory, and get rid of the less expensive items he was selling, because they no longer fit in with the image he was trying to project. To do this he started selling the other items on a second eBay account.

The first month he made the change, John said he "had nightmares waiting to see what would happen." Sales started picking up, slowly at first, but he was getting a few more sales, and at higher prices than he'd gotten in several years.

Over the next six months sales kept growing. John noticed a lot of new customers, along with many of the old ones starting to buy again.

One of the things John decided to do was move some of his business off of eBay, so he wouldn't be caught off guard like he was last time. This time he opened a Yahoo store, and got his designer to match its theme with his eBay store. The Yahoo store is making sales, but getting traffic to it is always a struggle.

John has tried Google AdWords, and adding special inserts in each of his mailings. He still has high hopes for the Yahoo store, but for now he knows real success there is probably still years off.

"If I could give sellers any advice," Johns says, "it is to hang in there, and be willing to do whatever it takes to succeed. Getting the consultant was the hardest thing I ever did, because up until that point I'd done it all myself. But, without them, I don't think I'd be here today.

"Don't be afraid to seek out help," John said. "It saved my business.

Jim – Part time eBayer

Jim calls himself a junker.

"For thirty-five years," he says, "I've gone to every auction and estate sale I can. I always seemed to walk away with several boxes of stuff, books, magazines, bric-a-brac, car parts, just about anything you can think of really.

"At the same time, I am one of those guys you see picking through your neighbor's trash, you know when they set out the furniture and everything, after they've cleaned out the attic or the garage. It's amazing the kind of things they throw away! I've gotten computers, printers, TV's, VCR's, even twenty or thirty dollars in cans several times.

"By 2009 I'd filled two garages, and a couple of sheds with all of this stuff. I think I'm one of those guys Frank and Mike from American Pickers would love to come across. I got old toys, milk bottles, bikes, you name it spread out everywhere.

"My wife passed away a few years ago, and it got me to thinking what would happen to all of this stuff if I wasn't here? I didn't want to stick the kids with having to get rid of it all.

"A neighbor told me about Craigslist, and I sold some of the furniture and TV's on there. It was all pretty easy, I just took a few pictures, wrote a couple lines about what I had, and put it out there. I got a lot of calls, and I probably made somewhere around $500 that first week and a half.

"That got me thinking about eBay. I'd purchased a few things there over the years. I figured it might be time to start selling some things, too.

"The first thing I sold was an old pedal car from the 1940's. It was well used and just starting to get some rust spots. Thirty-three people bid on it, and it sold for $427.00. I paid twenty bucks for it back in the early sixties."

Jim told me, "That sale got me really excited about selling on eBay."

He went on to describe a lot of his better sales, there were a lot of old toys, some silver dollars, and a lot of smaller things that went for just a few dollars. "Of course," Jim added, "there were also a lot of disappointments. Some things wouldn't sell no matter how much I lowered the price, and others I thought would sell for a whole lot, might just as well have not sold.

"But, overall," he said, "I really enjoy selling on eBay, and I make some good money, too. I also get the chance to meet a lot of interesting people. Many of them email to compliment me on the items I'm selling, or to tell me about something similar they had when they were growing up.

"Other times, when I wasn't sure what it was that I was selling, someone would email me and tell me what it was, or that I spelled the name wrong. Every time they gave me more details" he said, "I'd update my listing, and many times I'd get more bids, because now I had it listed properly."

Jim is seventy-three now, and he still enjoys selling on eBay, although he has started to slow down the number of items he lists. He has a few hundred items in his eBay store, and adds fifteen or twenty items per week.

Sarah – eBay education specialist

S arah got her start on eBay like a lot of people, buying stuff. She enjoys reading history and science fiction, and eBay offered her an unending supply of new books. Her first year on eBay she probably bought seventy-five books. She also found herself buying DVD's for the kids, and occasionally some clothes.

The selling bug caught her late in 2006. After completing her one hundredth eBay transaction, she told herself, "Why not give selling a shot?"

At first, she started selling back some of the books she had originally bought on eBay. Another time she cleaned out the garage, and decided that rather than doing her yearly garage sale, she would sell those items on eBay. Sarah says, "That sale netted me $327.12. My friends didn't believe me when I told them what I made but pretty soon, several of them were asking me if I could sell a few items for them, too."

She sold an electric guitar for one friend and got a whopping $1225.00. Another time she sold a cameo and some old jewelry for $373.00. After that everyone in the neighborhood was asking her to sell an item for them, or asking her for advice on how they could become eBay sellers, too.

In a six month period Sarah helped three of her friends get started selling on eBay. As time went on she spent more time helping friends learn how to sell. Sarah really enjoyed teaching people how to sell. To do a better job of it she started reading pretty much every book she could get her hands on about selling on eBay.

In early 2009 she learned about eBay University, and the eBay Educational Specialists program. That really intrigued her. Sarah spent some time exploring the program. She talked to some of the instructors listed in the directory and was lucky enough to find a lady who lived close to her who was willing to sit down with her, and answer a lot of the questions she had about the program. Sarah ended up taking one of the classes a few weeks later, and that really sold her on the program.

What Sarah liked about the Educational Specialists Program was it provided her with a structured way to present information to her students. Another plus was the fact she was provided with a Power Point presentation to supplement the information she gave in her classes, and there was an optional workbook she could provide students to help them learn.

She's been teaching classes for four years now, and says she learns as much from the students as they do from her. "It always surprises me," says Sarah. "They have some really great ideas about what to sell, and most of them are always so excited to get started."

One of the things she really enjoys is working with seniors. "Many of them are still coming to grips with how to use a computer, but that doesn't stop them from wanting to learn more about how they can buy and sell items on eBay.

"I had this one lady several years ago," she said. "She was so excited to learn how to sell because she wanted to make some extra money to help her granddaughter pay her way through college. And, I was just so touched because here's this sixty-three year old grandmother who'd never used a computer until three months ago, and now she wanted to make some money at it for such a great cause."

"I've probably helped several dozen moms over the years who've wanted to break away from their jobs so that they could stay home with their kids while they were growing up."

"Because of eBay," she continued, "I'm doing what I always wanted to do - Helping people!"

Barb – eBay newbie

Barb is new to eBay.

By day Barb is a pretty young assistant manager at a woman's clothing store, and is hoping to become a manager in the next twelve to eighteen months. Because she's new on the job money is a little tight right now, and she's hoping she can make a consistent $500.00 per month on eBay so she can buy a new car.

Last month she made $225.00 on $500.00 in sales, so she's about half way there.

She's only been selling on eBay for about two months, and is still trying to figure the whole thing out. She's got about fifty sales under her belt now.

Most of her sales have been women's and children's clothes she picked up at Good Will and other thrift stores. She's familiar with fashion because of her job, so Barb has a good idea of what brands and styles are in demand. She's thinking of buying a lot of the closeouts where she works and trying her luck selling them, but she's afraid it might create a conflict of interest if anyone finds out.

Last week she picked up some good deals at T. J. Maxx and Kohl's, and is hoping to make some good money there.

How to price the items she sells is one of Barb's biggest concerns. Up until now she has been starting all of her auctions out at double what she paid for them.

The problem is: Quite a few of her items are being snapped up within a few hours of when she lists them by people who use the buy-it-now option. Another forty percent of her items aren't moving at all, even when she lowers the price.

Last week Barb tried to tweak some of her prices. She picked out seven items she thought would sell really well, and decided she would start the bidding at four times what she paid. Five of her items sold with buy-it now, even with the higher prices. One sold at the starting price, and the other one didn't get any bids at all.

Barb was pretty excited with the results of her pricing experiment. She is going to continue stretching her prices and see what happens.

Another thing worrying Barb is what to do with her unsold items. She can't afford to keep relisting them as auctions because of the fees, but she's not sure that she's ready for an eBay store, either.

For now, Barb plans to keep selling everything at auction, while she does a little more research on eBay stores. She wants to make sure it's the right move for her.

Davis – High School Student

Davis is still a senior in high school. No one would know that from looking at his eBay store.

Davis has been selling on eBay for just over nine months. After three months of selling on eBay, he opened an eBay store. He used some of his profits and had a professional designer layout his eBay store and selling template.

He wants me to stress he's not a millionaire – YET!

Right now he makes about a thousand dollars a month, and he's fine with that. He bought a 2002 Mustang convertible last week, with cash. "How many high school seniors can say that?"

He sells Manga and Anime. And, business is booming.

"I started out by selling some of the books in my collection," says Davis. "I've got over 1200 books in my collection, and it's still growing. I've also got 63 DVD's – Death Note, Yugio, Bleach, Naruto, and more.

"The way I got started was, I wanted to get The Walking Dead Collection, and I didn't have sixty bucks, so I got mom to let me sell some stuff on her eBay account. Before I knew it, I had a hundred bucks the first week, and I had close to that again the next week.

"After four weeks of this I talked mom into letting me get my own eBay account, and the first thing I did was open an eBay store.

"In two weeks I had two hundred books and twenty-five DVD's for sale in my eBay store. After that I started talking with some of my friends about what I was doing, and a lot of them sold me some of the stuff they didn't want any more. A few of them even just gave me the stuff, and said 'Good Luck!'

"It's been a lot of fun," said Davis, "and one of the reasons I think my items are selling so well is I really know my stuff. I've read most of these series. Unlike a lot of the bigger sellers, I don't just go with the catalog description. I write my own reviews, and try to tell people how cool the stories and characters are. I don't give any spoilers or anything like that, but I let people know I'm excited, and I'm sure they will be too, if they read the books, or watch the DVD's.

"How cool is that! I get to work with the stuff I love, and I can read all of the books before I mail them."

Davis plans on dominating eBay's Manga and Anime categories before he graduates from high school. He's already set his sights on Amazon, and his own website.

Terry - Automobile internet manager

Terry has been the Internet Manager at a small town Chevy dealership for nearly ten years.

Most of his job involves responding to customer emails about cars listed on the dealer's website, and calling potential customers to book appointments for the salesmen. Occasionally he is called upon to post some banners on the website, or fill in as a salesman if they are short of people.

Several of the salesmen have posted cars on eBay for the dealership over the years. Most of the time the cars they listed were fixer uppers that would have been sold at auction otherwise. The problem is, because the cars were fixer uppers, many of them had rust or mechanical problems, that weren't described really well. As a result, the dealership had ten sales with a 2.5 overall feedback rating.

In 2011 the dealership got a new sales manager. The dealership he came from had a major presence on eBay, and one of the new responsibilities he assigned Terry was getting the dealership's inventory on the site.

Other than buying a few movies now and then, Terry had no idea how eBay worked. One of the first things he did was call customer service at eBay for some pointers. They gave him some good advice, and suggested a few places he could go for help.

Terry also called the internet manager at his sales manager's old dealership, and he received several great ideas to help him get started.

One of the things Terry decided was to open a new eBay account in the dealership's name. He didn't want to have to battle bad feedback when he was just starting out.

They had a number of options starting out. Several of the providers he found had the ability to post their entire inventory on eBay and Craigslist. The dealership decided they didn't want to try that especially when they were just getting started with eBay. The costs would have been over $2000 per month between their eBay store fees and the service provider's charges.

Management was also unsure whether they wanted to put their new car selection on eBay. The thought was they would have had to show major discounts to generate any interest there.

The final decision was to start out slow and only list special cars on eBay. The first week Terry listed a 1978 El Camino, a 1982 Trans Am, and an old Ford four wheel drive pickup.

Of the three, the Ford pickup was the only one to sell.

As the dealership listed and sold more cars on eBay, it refined its strategy. They got a better idea about what type of cars would sell to eBay customers, and which ones they should steer clear of listing on the site.

Two years after getting started they've sold fifty-seven cars on eBay. In that same time, they've listed one hundred and fifty-two cars, so they're selling about one-third of the cars they try to sell.

They also worked out a great system for choosing which cars to list on eBay. Right off they decided against trying to sell any auction block specials. Time has shown them that the best cars to sell on eBay are something special or unique. Old sports cars sell very well in any condition, the same goes for just about any type of four wheel drive pickups in the $6000 to $10,000 price range. They've also had some good luck with luxury cars, and have sold a few Porsche's, Infinity's, and a Lexus, or two.

Terry has also sold two boats, a "big ass" RV, and several motorcycles the dealership has taken in trade.

Going forward they want to expand their eBay sales, and are watching the papers and local auctions for cars they think would be a good fit for their business.

Terry says he would recommend eBay for any dealership. "It's a great way to increase sales, but it also means you need to be prepared to work with online customers. We are in Iowa, and many of our customers come from Minnesota, Wisconsin, Missouri, and even as far away as California or New York.

"You need to coordinate financing and titling for them. And, because many of them are flying in just to pick up their new car, you need to be sure everything is ready for them when they get there. One time we sold a Nissan 370 Z to Canada, and the paperwork dragged out for weeks. Finally we told them it was ready, and they had their driver on the way to pick it up, when we discovered we needed another paper. We got it taken care of at the last minute with Fed Ex, but it could have really caused some problems because of the distance they had to travel.

"My advice is: Take every sale that you can. But make sure everyone is on board before you get started. You need the cooperation of finance, management, sales people, and your titling department. Everyone has to be willing to work together."

Bonus Excerpt
Freaking Idiots Guide to Fiverr

(If you've ever thought of selling services online, Fiverr is hands down the easiest site to get started on. Tens of thousands of people have discovered Fiverr is a great way to make it big, five bucks at a time. These are the first two chapters to my book, Freaking Idiots Guide to Fiverr).

In the beginning …

Fiverr is a freelance website where sellers list a gig (any service – crazy ass or otherwise) they are willing to provide for five bucks!

The cool part is, everything on Fiverr is priced at $5.00, not a penny more, or less – MAYBE! (but we'll get to that part a little later). I know what you're thinking – Five bucks! That's crazy! Who's going to do anything for five bucks anymore? But, you'd be surprised.

When the time came for me to purchase my first Kindle book cover, I couldn't afford to pay $300 to $500 for a professional graphic designer, so I figured what the hell? I dropped five bucks on a Fiverr.

Now I'm a serial Fiverr!

That five bucks led to me spending $190 in my first 20 days on the site. It's addictive. It's fun. And, it's just crazy what all of these people are willing to do for only five bucks.

***

Here are just a few things you might not know about Fiverr.

1) Fiverr was launched in February 2010.

2) It was founded by Micha Kaufman and Shai Wininger.

3) All gigs are priced at $5.00.

4) Sellers receive $3.93 for each completed gig (Fiverr's take is $1.00, and PayPal fees grab another 8 cents).

5) As of January 2013, there are over 1,000,000 gigs listed on Fiverr.

6) According to Alexa, Fiverr is ranked the top 195th site in the world, and 185th in the United States.

7) In 2011 and 2012 alone, Fiverr received over $20 million in venture capital financing

8) Every gig on Fiverr starts out with the words "I will [fill in the blank] for $5.00."

What can you sell on Fiverr?

What can you sell on Fiverr?

Perhaps a better question is what can't you sell on Fiverr? A quick look at the website shows people offering a number of normal and not so normal services.

Before we even try to pin down any ideas for what you should sell, let's take a look at some of the crazy ass shit on Fiverr that is selling well.

1) There's this middle aged dude (anibalf). His offer is to sing a depressing Happy Birthday as a mouse. In what you can see of

his cover video there's an old dude wearing a Mickey Mouse hat and he really does seem to be depressed. Any guesses how many of these he's sold over the last year? 107! That's 107 people shelling out five bucks each to see a depressing old man sing the Happy Birthday song in a Mickey Mouse Hat.

2) Jebediahjenkins will do anything you want (within reason) as a redneck for $5.00. His cover photo shows this redneck geek in a cowboy hat in front of a confederate flag. He can sing, play his "geetar," and even deliver a special "redneck-ified" message. For $10.00 more he will do it outdoors, and for $20.00 he will rush deliver this video extravaganza in only two days instead of the normal five. And, in case you were wondering, he's sold 67 gigs in the last seven months.

3) And, there is this girl – (ragcloll). She will "write your name, link or any words" on her "sexy butt." Get this – You even get to choose the color of her sexy thong (for a $20.00 gig extra). Add another $20.00, and she will have her friend join her for two sexy butt messages. She's sold 35 gigs in less than four months. She also offers a similar "boob" gig that shows 67 sales in the last five months.

4) (Extrainput) offers to "distribute 30 flyers in New York City or around Baruch College." He has numerous gig extras, and offers photo proof that the job is actually done. A few of the gig extras include: Print and handout 100 color flyers $20.00, move it up to 300 flyers for $50.00. Business appears to be booming as he has delivered on 592 gigs in six months. I've seen two other guys offering similar services in Chicago and Philadelphia. Both of them have collected over 150 gigs.

5) This one may top them all for sheer craziness. (mdlasky) offers to "record an Xmas greeting or anything else as Jesus." The man has some really crazy pictures to enhance the listing. He has sold 682 gigs in the last year. And, yes – he will graciously accept tips for Jesus in his "tip jar."

6) This one hasn't gotten many takers, but maybe it will help you come up with some ideas. (madame_marie) offers to cast a psychic spell "giving you bigger boobs." Perhaps we can find one like this for guys, but aimed a little lower?

7) (drewapple) will "draw you a penis for $5.00." The offer is to draw you a "cute or funny or ugly or scary or kawaii or realistic or fantastic penis." Some of them even have faces or beards. Not a big mover yet, but it's only been a gig for two weeks.

8) Perhaps a professional video testimonial is more to your liking. (Screamingfinger) has collected 1111 gigs in the last year for his offer to "give you a video testimonial with/out business suit." He offers five gig extras for from $10.00 to $40.00. (Banjoman15) has a similar offer to "give a real looking testimonial" for which he has collected 744 gigs. He can also promote your product as Albert Einstein.

9) Everyone dreams about being rich someday. This offer from (nogalicious) is to meditate on your "financial abundance for five minutes straight." According to the gig details page "windfalls are not uncommon," and she invites tips based upon your good fortune – a "3% to 10% tip" to be exact. I'd laugh, but she's collected 291 gigs on this one in the last two years. Another gig from this woman will help you get pregnant. And, just in case

you still have a problem, she has a gig extra on this one offering her top five fertility tips for only $5.00.

Are you beginning to get the idea?

There is no limit to the type of gig you can offer. If you can imagine it, you can do it.

Read These Books Next

eBay for Dummies by Marsha Collier. (Like all of the Dummies books, this one is a fun, easy read, and gives you a lot of great info to boot. You will find this especially helpful if you're new to eBay selling.

eBay 101: Selling on eBay for Part-time or Full-time Income by Steve Weber. Weber has written books about how to sell on all of the major online markets, eBay, Amazon, and Etsy. Another of his books, Barcode Booty, will show you how you can find items to sell in retail stores, thrift shops, library sales, and more, simply by using your cell phone and a barcode scanner.

eBay Power Seller Secrets: Insider Tips Form eBays Most Successful Sellers by Brad Schepp and Debra Schepp. This book helped me a lot back when I first started selling on eBay. A lot of the information is dated now, but you should still be able to pick up some useful tips.

Good Sellers, Bad Buyers: Protecting Yourself on eBay by Lexie Thornton. I just picked this book up during a free promotion last week. Learn how to protect yourself in everything you do on eBay from writing descriptions to shipping. I would strongly recommend this book.

eBay Photography the Smart Way by Joseph T. Sinclair and Stanley Livingston. This book will help you nail photographing any type of item for eBay. If you want to sell more items, better pictures are a sure way to draw more bidders.

How to Start and Run an eBay Consignment Business by Skip McGrath. This book is from 2006 so some of the information is going to be outdated, but if you are interested in selling items for other people, you can learn a lot from this book.

Easy HTML for eBay by Nicholas Chase. One thing that can help every eBay seller spruce up their listings is a basic understanding of html (the computer language used to build web pages). Another bonus is it's available for just one penny on Amazon.

Turn eBay Data Into Dollars by Ina Steiner. Ina Steiner, (a co-founder of the *eComerce Bytes Blog*) scored a homerun with this book. Once again, I have to tell you that some of the information provided is dated, but if you really want to understand how to apply data to auction pricing and selling, this is the best book available on the subject.

Tax Loopholes For eBay Sellers: Pay Less Tax and Make More Money by Diane Kennedy and Janelle Elms. Tax laws have changed since this book was published but it will give you a lot of ideas you probably never thought of about how your part time eBay business can help you save big money on taxes.

Before you go

Thank you for reading this book. If you enjoyed it, or found it helpful, I'd be grateful if you'd post a short review. Your review really does help. It helps other readers decide if this book would be a good investment for them, and it helps me to make this an even better book for you. I personally read all of the reviews my books receive, and based on what readers tell me, I can make my books even better, and include the kind of information readers want and need.

Thanks again for choosing my book, and here's wishing you great success in your writing.

Amazon page: amazon.com/author/nickvulich

Blog: http://www.indieauthorstoolbox.com/

Email: hi@nickvulich.com

Books by Nick Vulich

eBay 2014: Why You're Not Selling Anything on eBay, and What you Can Do About it

Freaking Idiots Guide to Selling on eBay: How Anyone Can Make $100 or More Everyday Selling on eBay

Sell it Online: How to Make Money Selling on eBay, Amazon, Fiverr, & Etsy

How to Make Money Selling Old Books & Magazines on eBay

eBay Subject Matter Expert: 5 Weeks to becoming an eBay Subject Matter Expert

Indie Authors Toolbox

Audio Books by Nick Vulich

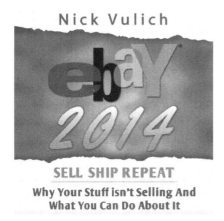

eBay 2014: Why Your Stuff Isn't Selling And What You Can Do About It

Freaking Idiots guide to Selling on eBay: How anyone can make $100 or more everyday selling on eBay

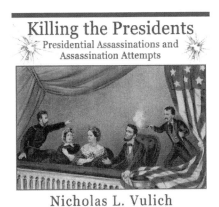

Killing the Presidents: Presidential Assassinations and
Assassination Attempts

Manage Like Abraham Lincoln